Tongue Twisters

Tough tongue twisters for kids

Table of Contents

Introduction 1

Tough Tongue Twisters 2

Conclusion 33

Introduction

Thank you for taking the time to pick up this book, containing hundreds of different tongue twisters that will challenge people of all ages!

Some of these tongue twisters look easy on paper, but when you try to say them out loud... Oh boy they can be tricky!

Test your skills and the skills of your family and friends with the tricky tongue twisters within. If you find a tongue twister particularly easy, just try to repeat it a few times quickly and it will be sure to challenge you!

This book is sure to provide hours of challenging fun for the whole family. Enjoy trying these testing tongue twisters today!

Once again, thanks for choosing this book, I hope you enjoy it!

Tough Tongue Twisters

Peter Piper picked a pack of pickled peppers.

A pack of pickled peppers Peter Piper picked.

How much wood would a woodchuck chuck, if a woodchuck could chuck wood?

She sells seashells by the seashore.

Becky bought a bit of butter but the butter Becky bought was bitter.

Can you imagine an imaginary menagerie manager managing an imaginary menagerie?

This black bug bled blue-black blood while the other black bug bled blue.

Shy Shelley says she shall sew sheets.

Sam's shop stocks short spotted socks.

I saw Susie sitting in a shoe-shine shop.

She shines where she sits and she sits where she shines.

Round the rough and rugged rock the ragged rascal rudely ran.

Robert ran rings around the Roman ruins.

Six sick hicks nicked six slick bricks with picks and sticks.

Seventy-seven benevolent elephants.

One-one was a racehorse.

Two-two was one too.

One-one won one race.

Two-two won one too!

Six sleek swans swam south swiftly.

Anne and Andy's anniversary is in April.

I thought I'd thought of thinking of thanking you.

He threw three free throws.

Willie's really weary.

I wish to wash my Irish wristwatch.

Tom threw Tim three thumbtacks.

Nine nice nurses nursing nicely.

Which witch is which?

Find four fine fresh fish for friends.

Three thin thinkers thinking thick thoughtful thoughts.

Two tried and true tridents.

Black background. Brown background.

Tie twine to three tree twigs.

Three short sword sheaths.

Rolling red wagons.

Green glass globes glow greenly.

The queen in green screamed.

Six slimy snakes slithered silently.

Lesser leather never weathered wetter weather better.

Fred fed Ted bread and Ted fed Fred bread.

Which wristwatches are Swiss wristwatches?

I slit the sheet, the sheet I slit, and on the slitted sheet I sit.

He threw three balls.

We're real rear wheels.

Race runners really want red wine right away.

Two tiny tigers took two taxis to town.

Willies really weary.

Tommy Tucker tried to tie Tammy's turtle's tie.

Double bubble gum doubles bubbles.

A slimy snake slithered down the sandy Sahara.

She said she should sit.

I wish a fish were in my dish.

I'm not the fig picker or the fig picker's son.
But I'll pick figs until the fig picker comes.

If you notice this notice you will notice that this notice isn't worth noticing.

Five frantic frogs fled from fifty fierce fish.

Silly sheep weep and sleep.

Shut the shutters and sit in the shop.

Bake big batches of bitter brown bread.

Whoever slit the sheets is a good sheet slitter.

Many mummies make money.

An elephant was asphyxiated in the asphalt.

Fresh fried fish.

Fish fresh fried.

Fried fish fresh.

Fish fried fresh.

There is a minimum of cinnamon in the aluminum pan.

A lump of red leather, a red leather lump.

Preshrunk silk shirts.

Swan swam over the sea.

Swim swan, swim!

Swan swam back again.

Well swum swan!

You know New York.

You need New York.

You know you need unique New York.

Blake's black bike's back break broke.

Each Easter Eddie eats eight Easter eggs.

The batter with butter is the batter that is better.

The sandwich on the sand was sent by the sane witch.

Twelve twins twirled twelve twigs.

Clowns grow glowing crowns.

Richard's wretched rachet wrench.

If two witches watched two watches then which watch would which witch watch?

The soldier's shoulder surely hurts.

She surely sees seas slapping shores.

Six sick sea-serpents swam the seven seas.

A proper cup of coffee from a proper copper coffee pot.

Blue glue gun, green glue gun.

Five fat friars frying five flying fish.

Picky Peter picks packs of peanuts.

Thin sticks, thick bricks.

Six slick slippers sliding south.

People peacefully pledge plenty of pennies.

Real rear wheel.

Flies fly but fat flies fry.

This shop stocks sport socks with spots.

No need to light a night-light on a night like tonight.

A real rare whale's rear.

Ken Dodd's dad's dog's dead.

Bug's black blood, black bug's blood.

A quick-witted cricket critic quit quickly.

The cat crept in the crypt, crapped and crept out.

Dear mother, give your other udder to my other brother's brother.

Certified certificates from certified certificate certifiers.

What noise annoys a noisy oyster?

Freddy is ready to roast red roaches.

Wayne washed Washington's white washing when Washington's washer went West.

Suzie sits shining silver shoes.

Mumbling bumbling, bumbling mumbling.

Of all the felt I ever felt, I never felt felt that felt like that felt felt.

Thirty-six thick silk sheets.

The sixth sick sheik's sheep slept.

Crash quiche cooking course.

Who holds Joe Blow's nose when Joe blows his nose?

Six Czech cricket critics.

It's a nice night for a white rice fight.

Real brown round bread.

Chill, shake, serve.

How many ducks could a duck duct tape, if a duck could duct tape ducks?

Mister Twister's tongue twisters twist tongues.

Six sick sticky skeletons.

Chip shop chips.

Real loyal royal lawyer.

Free Ritz wristwatch.

Six sick slick slender saplings.

Thin teeth taste thick meat.

Ken's cat can't keep calm.

Which Swiss witch switched the Swiss wristwatches.

I miss my Swiss Miss.

How much squash could a sasquatch squish if a sasquatch could squish squash.

It dawned on Don at dawn.

A snake sneaks to seek a snack.

A synonym for cinnamon is a cinnamon synonym.

The rural ruler ruled rurally.

Willy went wild when his wooden whistle wouldn't work.

If a dog chews shoes, who's shoes does he chew?

Darla's dollars don't discriminate.

Green and brown blades of grass.

Sleep sweetly. Sleep sweetly. Sleep sweetly.

The greedy Greek geek agreed.

Floyd flicks fat fleas for a fixed flat fee.

An inchworm inches on ivy that itches.

The burger burglar burgled beautiful burgers.

Sophie snapped a selfie with her silver cell phone.

She surely suits shiny sleek short skirts.

How many pounds in a groundhog's mound when a groundhog pounds hog mounds?

A happy hippo hopped and hiccupped.

Yelling yellow yeti.

Six skunks sat on trunks.

Truly rural. Truly rural. Truly rural.

Which witch is which?

Willy's real rear wheel.

Cooks carefully cook cupcakes quickly.

Really leery, rarely Larry.

A blue bluebird bit Barry.

Friendly fleas and fireflies.

I scream, you scream, we all scream for ice cream!

Sally swims slowly so she shall not sink.

Sally solemnly sat in silence.

Pirate's private property.

Santa's short suit shrunk.

Mary Mac's mother's making Mary Mac marry me.

Four furious friends fought.

Three short sword sheaths.

Singing Sammy sung songs on sinking sand.

Eddie edited everything.

Cheetahs chew chunks of cheap cheddar cheese.

Pad kid poured curd pulled cod.

Brisk brave brigadiers brandished broad bright blades.

How many clams can you cram in a clean clam can?

Rory the warrior and Roger the worrier were reared wrongly.

The thirty-three thieves thought they thrilled the throne throughout Thursday.

What noise annoys an oyster?

An annoying noise annoys an oyster.

Peter the pianist played the piano peacefully.

I saw a kitten eating chicken in the kitchen.

Red leather yellow leather.

Keeping customers content creates kingly cash.

Ensuring excellence isn't easy.

Feel free to follow that fellow forward.

Time takes terrible toll on intentions.

Rubber baby buggy bumpers.

Susie's sister sewed socks for soldiers.

An ape ate eight grape cakes.

A tutor who tooted the flute tutored two tooters to toot.

Six thick thistle sticks.

Top shops stock chopsticks.

Ten tense teens slowly toasted toast.

Conclusion

Thanks again for choosing this book!

I hope you had fun trying out these tricky tongue twisters and sharing them with your family and friends!

www.ingramcontent.com/pod-product-compliance
Lightning Source LLC
LaVergne TN
LVHW021744060526
838200LV00052B/3472